Hidden Streams

Reflections from a Desert Oasis

Bishop "Skip" McDonald

ISBN 978-0-578-27971-8

To Ginny, my wife and best friend.

Intro

I recently returned from a nine-day trip to Atlanta and Tybee Island, Georgia, to visit an old friend and to celebrate the life of his sister-in-law. While there, I was introduced to a unique Southern dish that the locals refer to as a "low country boil"—a delicious combination of fresh Atlantic shrimp, crab, andouille sausage, red potatoes, chopped carrots and corn on the cob. Upon returning to my home in Arizona I realized that this manuscript, Hidden Streams, was a literary version of a low country boil; a potpourri of personal poetry, life reflections and renegade prayers—all thrown together in an attempt to try to come up with something that had diversity but did not lack in flavor. It is my sincere wish, as the "word chef," that you will find the following chapters both enjoyable and nourishing.

Bon Appétit!

*My first name, Bishop, is a given name and not a clerical designation. It was passed down to me from my father and has provided me with preferred parking at the Salt Lake City Airport, as well as raising more than a few eyebrows at both Catholic and Episcopal gatherings.

Searching

How is it that I stop to admire the radiance of rainbows yet not even begin to recognize the beauty of the integrated colors of our shared humanity?

Where do I ever find the time to judge the motivations and actions of others when I have entire courtrooms of my own issues that need to be put on trial?

Why is it that I hold onto grudges, clutching them like a bag full of precious jewels that I hope will somehow enhance my personal value and add some sparkle to my self-worth?

Aren't these remembered hurts just jagged lumps of coal that have become deeply lodged within the concealed caverns of my mind and heart?

They should be patiently extracted and then gently tossed into the transformative fires of forgiveness and reconciliation.

Why does my life sometimes feel like an ongoing banquet of half-baked ideas being served up with large helpings of overcooked regrets?

Televisions

Televisions, tell me your visions,
not the marketing decisions,
nor the formulated incisions into our senses,
now dulled to the miraculous,
while your talking heads seek out the disastrous.

We, the brand loyal soldiers of senseless greed,
watch your thirty second spots, blemishes indeed!

Cars, skin creams, tight abs; everyone dreams,
while the lost souls ride the remote control beams,
to be with the evening suitor,
the after-work mind looter,
the hypnotic time stealer,
the peering eye product dealer.

Televisions, tell me your visions.

Can We?

What search engines will we use to reach one another?

Will what we question bring forth revealing responses or will we remain password protected and fire-walled behind the naked fear of self disclosure?

Will you trust that I only wish to blend my truth with yours and see if we are drawing our mutual sustenance from the same well?

Can we surf this inner net together, dive below the surface of all the chatter and emerge to float freely on the calm and buoyant seas of Universal Love?

Will our search engines take us to places where we can see and hear and feel that power?

Will you meet me there often and tell me when there are times when you are too weak or too afraid to even try?

Can we travel between the heavenly realms and our earthly homes with both ease and humility?

Will we be able to freely give away what we have learned and not be tempted to revel in our own revelations?

If secrets are the weeds in the gardens of self-doubt, can we uproot them and plant the seeds of self-acceptance and mutual trust in their place?

Can we tenderly listen and embrace the weaknesses that we find in each other and avoid using them as platforms to display our own strengths?

Can we, at least this day, unplug our electronic devices and tune in with attentive ears to truly hear each other's dreams and desires, fears and failures?

I will wait for you outside of these digital walls, will you meet me there soon?

Discovering

It appears that my ego seems to find great pleasure in
hauling around my most hurtful memories,
dragging them along wherever I go,
like so many tattered and useless bags packed full of
resentments and unforgiveness.

Religious debates can often appear to be a gathering of well-intentioned cocoons attempting to explain the unique characteristics of butterflies.

Those who choose to sit on the fence of life eventually become entangled in the barbed wires of complacency.

Wisdom rides on the currents of the heart,
not on the tracks of the mind.

Sneaker Waves

They hide in the circulating currents of vast oceans, irregular beats in their pulsing hearts that appear on the surface to be so soothingly rhythmic. The ice-cold fury of their messages can instantly sweep over the unsuspecting souls of us who have been thrown off balance by the curved wet arms of dark and distant memories, now reawakened.

My talents are gifts with legs that follow me,
even when I foolishly try to run away from them.

True friendships are like finely tuned muscles—they offer both strength and support, however they can quickly atrophy if not engaged often enough.

The problem with holding onto grudges is that they always feel obligated to hold us back.

Every time I take small bites out of my ego
I find that I am better able to swallow my pride.

I am just getting too old to continue to annoy myself.

Awakening

As dawn approaches, my thoughts seem to scatter
like a flock of frightened sparrows
rising up from the branches of my awakening imagination.

They fly in search of a quieter place to roost,
beyond the swirling winds of doubt and uncertainty
and into the pre-dawn light that is now illuminating
the verdant forests of dreams and promises
that this new day is calling forth.

A Morning Walk

The gentle breezes,
cooled by a dancing mountain stream,
brought to me the fragrances of an early summer morning,
awakening my soul to a surrounding symphony.

The wild Canada geese lead me forward,
a harsh and confident cadence,
the sounds of hundreds of rusty feathered hinges,
pointing the way in perfect formation.

As I step slowly into a meadow of melodious songs,
soft, yet penetrating,
I find it alive with the quiet roar of sunlight
now illuminating the unfolded wings of radiant monarchs
perched upon their thrones of flowering thistles.

A lone osprey offers up a shrill and lofty introduction,
calling me, once again, to immerse myself completely
in this open air orchestra of audible Grace.

If you are uncertain as to your direction in life,
a good place to start might be to consult
the map of your own motivations.

Denial is merely a state of mind that has surrendered to the power of fear and then trained to behave like the truth.

This Iron Feather

(October 06, 2006)

I came out today,
not with a shout, but with a whisper.

The burden of carrying this iron feather has now been lifted
in the presence of those that I love.

I am not straight,
I am not crooked,
I am not happy,
I am not sad.

I am, however, unable to shrink my reality so that it can fit
comfortably into someone else's definition of me.

Labels belong on objects that cannot or will not change.

Release yourself to embrace transition,
for she is your friend, my friend.

This iron feather has now been transformed and transferred
from the cage of my own consciousness and onto the
currents of the immense possibilities that we can now share
together.

I came out today.

May silence become one of my closest friends
and not just a distant relative that
I allow to come and visit me on occasion.

I wish not so much to seek out certainty in my life as much as I desire to live authentically in the presence of uncertainty.

I must learn to close the doors of my past without regret, to look through the windows of my future without fear, and to unwrap the present that it is.

Happiness and humility are the barometers in our emotional lives that measure degrees of gratefulness.

The time that I spend fixating on the faults and flaws of others is always the same amount of time that I spend avoiding my own.

Faith is the force that allows the wild mustangs of my soul to kick down the self-imposed corrals of my own perceived limitations.

Any attempts to try to institutionalize spirituality will be as futile as trying to transport water in a paper bag.

When I walk into the Sacred Room,
the place where Spirit dwells,
I should take a deep breath,
hang up my frail ego on the coat rack of self-reflection,
then quietly gather together with others
to actively listen to the faint, but certain,
whisperings of the Great Mystery that surrounds us.

Speak not carelessly in the presence of the Infinite, for She will seek out conversation with another.

Listen not to the sister sirens of conformity and consumption, for their voices will become the static that will prevent you from hearing the faint footsteps of your true self drawing near.

Breathe not the stagnant air of convention, for it will not be able to sustain you along the path that leads to emotional and spiritual liberation.

Light is Spirit made visible.

Releasing

May your rest be gentle,
may your dreams dance with joy,
and may you awaken fresh to the glory
of the dawning of this new day.

Acadia

The sun rose hesitantly this morning,
slowly peaking over the ocean's edge,
as if contemplating, once again,
if this fragile island was deserving of her luminous glory.

With eyes closed,
I felt her caress my expecting soul,
an ever intensifying orgasm of light and warmth.

Her sister, the wind,
gently brought me the salty fragrance of a beach
awakened from a long night's rest.

And I?
I floated freely in a timeless capsule
of communion and bliss.

Lord, help me to navigate the river that is this day,
allow my heart not to sink in despair,
my mind not to be trapped in the turbulent tributaries
of untruth, and may my spirit flow freely
upon the currents of Your Love.

Truth is very much a fluid reality, although I foolishly try
to contain it. It desires and seeks to flow through me, while
the self-made dams of my own ego restrict its clear passage.
Guilt, on the other hand, is merely the hangover I suffer after
drinking too heavily from the polluted streams of
fearful thoughts and unforgiven offenses.

The sea makes love to the shore.
The expectant beach anxiously awaits
the long and gentle fingers of the incoming surf
to caress her sun soaked back
and then to massage the sandy curves and mounds
that she so willingly offers up.

Forgiveness is a process,
rarely an event.

Faith is the wick in the lantern of courage that,
when lit, will guide us through
our darkest times of doubt and despair.

Laughter is often the residual sound of a prayer that has been tickled.

Stay relaxed,
pay attention,
listen carefully,
speak honestly,
live openly.

Stay calm in tense situations;
a knot can not untie another knot.

The next time you peel back an onion, imagine that every layer that you expose is some past personal hurt, resentment, or unkind act that you have experienced on your life journey. The number of layers that you are willing to peel back will depend on how many tears you are willing to shed in the process.

Seek out the clarity of quiet.

Standing on the Shore

I see you standing on the shore of My love,
shed your layers of protection.

Come and emerge yourself in My liquid light
and allow Me to caress and to heal you.

Dive into My oceans and discover
the mirror image of yourself,
the reflection of the truth that lies deep within you.

Become a child once again
and know that this life is My gift to you.

Shed your doubts and fears
and gently unwrap the essence of your being.

I will be there.

Come and swim with My other creations,
for you are all one in different forms.

Your light will shine long after your lantern has vanished;
be not afraid.

Float freely on the surface
and allow My clouds to speak to your soul;
gaze upon My stars
and reflect upon those
who have traveled here before you.

You are light,
you are loved,
you are eternal.

I am here.

Dusk

Slowly descending curtain of faintest amber,
stitched loosely together
with wind-worn patches of billowy translucent clouds.

The soul-soliciting darkness gently approaches,
riding in on cool perfumed breezes of lavender and pine.

Summer leaves shimmer sporadically
on the stoic maples as shadows begin to appear,
summoning the day to come again and rest her head
gently upon the soft pillows of quiet blackness.

Within the celestial dressing room,
her nocturnal sister slowly steps
into a flowing velvet gown of deepest blue,
now adorned with the brightening glow of a billion stars.

May the tributaries of our collective wills always flow in the direction of the Divine stream of consciousness.

Loving

If I can remain grounded in love there is very little chance
that I will be uprooted by hate.

With all of our universal differences,
at least we all smile in the same language.

Gratitude is the rain that waters the gardens of compassion.

When the cold winds of uncertainty blow through the cracks in the caverns of my soul, Lord, please shelter me.

When anger sweeps like wildfire across the forests of my faith, Lord, please shield me.

When the floods of unwanted memories crash onto the sands of my serenity, Lord, lift me to higher ground.

When You find me lost once again in the deserts of doubt and despair, Lord, lead me back to the clear and refreshing springs of your Eternal Love.

Spirit laughs at the attempts of the ego to discount
the reality of our immortality.

Celebrate variety,
dance with diversity,
embrace uncertainty,
hold on to nothing,
not even to love itself,
for even that has to be given away.

Love is for giving.

Made in United States
Troutdale, OR
06/24/2023

10762628R00075